S0-BTP-100

The Pleasure is Mine

Overcoming

the

Need to Please

Judy Coburn

© Copyright 2008, Judy Coburn

All Rights Reserved.

No part of this book may be reproduced, stored in a
retrieval system, or transmitted by any means,
electronic, mechanical, photocopying, recording,
or otherwise, without written permission
from the author.

Photography by Judy Coburn

ISBN: 978-0-6152-2282-0

Acknowledgments

My gratitude abounds to those I love, who have taught me so much as we live out our joyous and messy life: my husband, Steve; daughter, Courtnay; my two sons, Mike and Zack; and my grandchildren Marty, Lily and Carson; and my new family members, Graham, Serena and Koren. Also thanks to my mom, Lil, for her support and wisdom. I am grateful for the support and love of my sibs, Sharon, Kate, John, and Ernie.

Special thanks to my colleagues and guy friends who contributed to the Man's Bill of Rights: Steve, Paul, Pete, Mike W., Mike C., Zack, Bill, Rob, Sidney, Brent, and Kent. It created some lovely conversations, and I am wiser for your help. Thanks to Courtnay, a wise and wonderful woman, for her additions to the Woman's Bill of Rights.

Thanks to Stephanie Killeen at Integrative Ink and William Earle and his team at Accurance for their professionalism and patience.

I must also express my deepest gratitude to my clients, whom I love and respect. Our relationships have deepened my perspective and taught me a great deal. Your courageous work continues to inspire me.

Foreword

The old tenet for writers is to write what you know. I am writing about pleasing because I am a pleaser in recovery. There is the side of me that is healthy, happy, and giving—and then there is my insecure, "hope you like me side," which could give away the family farm for a smile.

Getting to know and love my pleasing side has been very important work for me.

Winston Churchill once said that "Men [and women] stumble over the truth from time to time, but most pick themselves up and hurry off as if nothing happened."

After many years, I have paused to have a second look. It has made all the difference to me, and I believe it can for you as well.

Sometimes my vibrant, healthy side wants to kick my needy side to the curb, but I know that my pleasing side holds important lessons and has some truth to tell.

Warm regards,
Judy Coburn

About This Book

The Pleasure Is Mine is divided into sections that can assist you in overcoming your need to please. The first step is identifying your pleasing behaviors and recognizing the difference between healthy giving and unhealthy pleasing.

The second step is appraising both your light and dark sides. Many people find addressing their dark side easier than claiming their light. Be gentle with yourself as you do this work. Stand tall. Be honest.

Take time with the section entitled INDEPENDENCE DAY. From this section forward, there are exercises to help you practice being assertive, establish or strengthen healthy relationships and create a healthy, vibrant you.

The book concludes with story time.

As you make your way out of the pleasing trap, use the activities in the appendix to help you celebrate your accomplishments and identify areas needing attention. I recommend using a special loose leaf notebook to collect finished activities and any other articles, journal pages, etc. that are meaningful to you.

Remember, this is a process, not a quick trip. You **can** reach your destination. While change happens gradually, you are likely to feel relief very soon.

Table of Contents

If I asked you to name all the things you love, how long would it take for you to name yourself?

PLEASING MORE
AND
ENJOYING IT LESS?

*"Your current safe boundaries were once
unknown frontiers."*

-Anonymous

I. THERE IS NO "I" IN PEOPLE PLEASING

Okay so there is an "i" but it is a little one. This book is dedicated to helping you recover yourself and discover that you are worth loving. It is a book focused on helping you overcome *unhealthy* pleasing and laying stake to your big "I."

People-pleasing people (PPP's) are the salt of the earth. They are good people who just want world peace, love, and three-part harmony. And for the most part, their desires are genuine. The world would not be nearly as, well, pleasing without them.

Somewhere along life's road, our ideals for world peace and three part-harmonies collided with our own needs. We may have been taught to deny ourselves and give to others, even giving others the coats off our backs. That is a beautiful concept and a beautiful act.

So then, what is the problem with being loving and giving? It sounds noble and sacrificing and may well be, but all good acts are not created equally. Depending on one's motives, our "good act" could indeed be noble and sacrificing—or it could be narcissistic and self-serving. It could create an unbalance that depletes our reserves, causing us to rely on external fillers, get sick, or get enraged. The question to ask yourself is does your doing and giving come from your abundance or your emptiness?

Sometimes folks get wrapped up in the idea that it is their job to be pleasing. We may be second-generation pleasers born to families where pleasing is not only the norm but also an expectation. From birth, we received the message that only in our doing could we be loveable. That message becomes deeply ingrained and is reinforced with every good deed. When we are pleasing we:

- Get to be viewed as the salt of the earth
- Get to receive people's gratitude
- Get to be admired for being selfless
- Get to enjoy feeling nice
- Get to pad our karma
- Get to experience the joy of giving

Sounds wonderful, right? No one can fault that kind of behavior. However...once we are out of the sunshine and the birds are through singing "Zippity Doo-dah," other rewards may be lurking in the shadows of pleasing. We may choose to be pleasing so that we:

- Get to be rescued (it is hard to confront nice)
- Get to manipulate
- Get to avoid our own issues

- Get to avoid confrontation
- Get to pass on responsibility for our own happiness
- Get to keep score
- Get to deny our dark side
- Get to play the victim
- Get to fill the "not enough" void

And we get to deny the smoldering mountain of molten anger we may be suppressing. Ever seen one of those scary movies that terrify you when the hero/shero turns out to be the master-minded predator whose beautiful smile has retractable fangs? That is the scariest kind of horror flick! Is it any less scary to deal with a person who embodies kindness and giving but is filled with rage? Wow, that is the stuff of fairy tale antagonists (think Big Bad Wolf in Grandma's clothing, or any witch who pretties up to trick someone).

When our cars are out of gas, they stop running until refueled. When we are empty, we may not stop to refuel ourselves with what we need: rest, introspection, play, etc. Instead we rely on quick fixes: caffeine, sugar, pleasing, etc.

"Hold it," you may say, "my pleasing exhausts not fills me." I want to invite you to entertain the notion that you are getting *something* from pleasing. The trick is to figure out what it is and create a healthier solution for filling up. It can be tough to face our emptiness. It can be tough to address our own needs. It is also freeing.

II. TAKING INVENTORY

(Are you talking to me?)

If you are immobilized by your pleasing, feel terrified about making decisions, and have serious difficulty making it through your day without guidance, I would encourage you to seek a therapist to provide you with support.

If you intend to read this book in order to create new ways of beating yourself up, shut the book now. I am not into the "ain't it awfuls" or the "ain't I awfuls." I want no part of that.

This book is lighthearted and loving in tone because it is seriously important to delight in you and find the humor that erupts while we are mucking through our humanity. It is intent on helping you create abundance so that your giving comes from a place of fullness rather than emptiness. Those of you moving forward in love and compassion, read on.

EXERCISE ONE

INSTRUCTIONS: Please rate how strongly you agree or disagree with each of the following statements by placing an X in the appropriate box.					
1. I don't get what I need.	Strongly Disagree	Disagree	Undecided	Agree	Strongly Agree
2. Others have more freedom than I do.	Strongly Disagree	Disagree	Undecided	Agree	Strongly Agree
3. I covet their freedom.	Strongly Disagree	Disagree	Undecided	Agree	Strongly Agree
4. I am embarrassed or ashamed to ask for help.	Strongly Disagree	Disagree	Undecided	Agree	Strongly Agree
5. I feel angry when asking for the help I need.	Strongly Disagree	Disagree	Undecided	Agree	Strongly Agree
6. I hold resentments.	Strongly Disagree	Disagree	Undecided	Agree	Strongly Agree
7. I am often taken for granted.	Strongly Disagree	Disagree	Undecided	Agree	Strongly Agree
8. I am easily manipulated.	Strongly Disagree	Disagree	Undecided	Agree	Strongly Agree
9. I rely on other's opinion of me.	Strongly Disagree	Disagree	Undecided	Agree	Strongly Agree
10. It is hard for me to say positive things about myself.	Strongly Disagree	Disagree	Undecided	Agree	Strongly Agree
11. It is hard for me to disagree with others.	Strongly Disagree	Disagree	Undecided	Agree	Strongly Agree

What do you think? Were most of your answers on the "agree" or "strongly agree?" Could you benefit by freeing up some life-space and compassion for you?

I wonder if mother and father birds ever look into the nest of cavernous mouths and tweet, "Calgon, take me away"? I have seen nursing mother dogs enveloped in a cloud of milk-seeking puppies rise and shake off any little suction cups still clinging and walk away for respite.

Demands on humans are high as well. There are corporate decisions to be made, deadlines to meet, lunches to pack, dinner plans to work out, boo-boos to kiss, shoes to tie, loved ones to console, mailings to be delivered, carpooling to coordinate, soccer games to attend, laundry to wash, diapers to fold, and let's not even consider lawn care and pets. Add the burden of pleasing, and you could be reaching critical mass.

Of course for many, the concept of lawn-care and laundry to do may be too wonderful to imagine. Here is the recurring theme of this book. Whatever your circumstances, *taking care of you is critical.* It is not a luxury.

"Most of the shadows of this life are caused by our standing in our own sunshine."

-Ralph Waldo Emerson

III. OKAY, I MIGHT BE A PLEASER...

Consider these scenarios (with a nod to Jeff Foxworthy):

If your theme song is, "I Did it Your Way" and you don't work at a fast food restaurant...you might be a pleaser.

If you make a mistake and berate yourself for hours...you might be a pleaser.

If you provide an act of service for someone and then remind the person of that fact a few dozen times...you might be a pleaser.

If you worry that the librarian may not approve of your book selections...you might be a pleaser.

If the boss says, "Someone left the coffee pot turned on yesterday" and you feel guilty even though you had the day off...you might be a pleaser.

If someone says, "You missed a great party last night" even though you spent ten minutes talking to him/her *at* that party…you might be a pleaser.

If you envy the person who draws the unlucky short straw in the office (short straw cleans the toilets) because he "won"… you might be a pleaser.

If you have not taken time for yourself in the last three months…you might be a pleaser.

If in public you are mild-mannered David Banner but at home turn into the Incredible Hulk…you might be a pleaser.

If you buy your favorite ice cream in gallons and never get a spoonful…you might be a pleaser.

If a person you consider powerful compliments a workmate and you feel despondent for the rest of the day/week/decade…you might be a pleaser.

If your dog died, your mother is in the hospital, your car isn't running, and those around you don't have a clue….you might be a pleaser.

If you feel guilty and/or irritated if someone brings you a small gift because you don't have something to give in return….you might be a pleaser.

If you receive unexpected free-time and have no concept of how to delight in it …you might be a pleaser.

If you feel spent, exhausted, discouraged, and listless at the end of the day… you might be a pleaser.

If you go through a list of all your friends and acquaintances and there is not one of them you would call just to vent …you might be a pleaser.

If you have said to yourself, "What about me? …you might be a pleaser.

If your heart longs for someone to say, "You matter" without you having to even lift your pinky.…you might be a pleaser.

Here is the truth: *You DO matter,* and you don't even have to lift a pinky.

Believing that you matter requires courageous solitary work. In the wonderful one-woman show, *The Search for Signs of Intelligent Life in the Universe* (Warren, 1999), Lily Tomlin says, "We are all in this alone."

No other human can do this work for you. Loving ourselves is our challenge. It is our metamorphosis. When we nurture and feed our own soul, we step up to take our rightful place in the universe, neither crowding others nor surrendering too much of ourselves.

IV. WHAT CONDITION MY UNCONDITIONAL IS IN

(So we've established that I am a pleaser. How bad is it, and where do I get the shot?)

EXERCISE TWO

As you continue to take your personal inventory, consider the following questions:

Does your life bring you joy? Explain.

Most times, more now-then before

What percent of the time are you truly happy?

50% → 75%

How often do you laugh in a day, week, or month?

I will start to count but
Maybe 5 in a day 25 in a wk
100 in month

What percent of the time do you worry in a day, week, or month?

less lately but at least once
a wk

What was the last thing you did for you?

Bought a suit

Do you remember the dreams you had when you were ten? What were they?

To establish a balance in my life, I need to ___think of others___ less and ___me___ more.

As I read my answers, my reaction is:

I am doing better then I was!

I would like to make changes in the following ways:

Continue to improve on taking care of myself

V.   BEING SELFLESS REQUIRES A SELF

Spiders spin webs to catch their prey. Once caught, the spider wraps a cozy little web afghan around its victim to keep it nicely shrouded in the spider pantry until suppertime.   Spiders are doing their jobs. That is how they survive.

People pleasers can attach so many strings to their good deeds that their victims get stuck as tight as a bug in a spider's casserole.

When we do that, our expectations are that we will feel loved.   Our expectations are that the receiver of our good deeds will reciprocate.   The trouble is that our "victims" don't always reciprocate.   Or, if they feel obligated, they may pay us back but serve up resentment and mistrust as a side order. That feels bad.

> "We should give as we would receive, cheerfully, quickly, and without hesitation; for there is no grace in a benefit that sticks to the fingers."
>
> — *Seneca, Roman statesman*

Since we feel badly, we may try to please harder and faster or indulge in our other favorite excesses. Soon, in that vicious cycle, we may subconsciously *hope* for a negative response in order to continue indulging in our excesses. "Poor misunderstood, underappreciated me. I am no stranger to pain. I must numb my pain and anger with a chocolate martini while shopping online for things I can't afford." And even while there is a payoff, it is not what we, in our heart of hearts, want.

In the book THE PATHWAY, therapist Laurel Mellin writes that our mantra should be, "I don't have to be perfect to be wonderful." For pleasers, I would add: "I don't have to be pleasing to be lovable."

I DON'T HAVE TO BE PLEASING TO BE LOVABLE!!!!! Say that daily again and again as you drive, as you walk, as you shower, and as you exercise. I don't have to be pleasing to be lovable. Grind that message in.

I don't have to be pleasing to be lovable. I don't have to be pleasing to be lovable. I don't have to be pleasing to be lovable. *I don't have to be pleasing to be lovable.*

Sing it out loudly; pound your fist on the table to emphasize every word. Write it down on huge newsprint. Write it over and over again on the first page of a new journal. Write it in the sand. Write it in the bubbles of your bath. Learn to say it in different languages, including sign language. Whisper it to yourself. Say it to yourself as you stand in the grocery store line.

I DON'T HAVE TO BE PLEASING TO BE LOVABLE!!!! I do not have to be pleasing to be lovable. I am lovable without doing a thing. Revolutionary stuff, this.

This message needs to be firmly implanted in your brain. The sooner it is, the sooner you will feel okay about taking care of yourself. The more we take care of our own needs, the less likely we are of using other people to fill up, and the more likely we are of ringing true with our acts of altruism. We will be able to be there for others without placing additional burdens on them by our expectations. We need to firmly grind in the notion that we are deserving of care and love. It is not a commodity that we have to purchase by doing and giving.

EVERYONE DESERVES TO BE LOVED. It should be as free as the air we breathe. It is our right as a human being. Up until now, we had the notion that love was something for which we had to barter and trade. It is not. It is free!

Many people would argue that self-love creates narcissistic, self-involved individuals. Narcissism is a great mechanism to prop up, massage, and place barriers around one's ego. While people-pleasing does not seem to be egotistical, it is related to narcissism in that they are both involved in the realm of self-absorption. Narcissism binds you. People-pleasing binds you. Self-love frees you. The difference between loving yourself and people-pleasing is shown below.

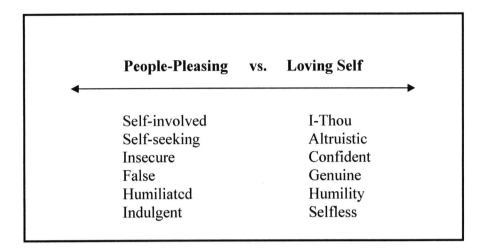

People-Pleasing vs. **Loving Self**

People-Pleasing	Loving Self
Self-involved	I-Thou
Self-seeking	Altruistic
Insecure	Confident
False	Genuine
Humiliated	Humility
Indulgent	Selfless

When you truly love yourself, you don't need the external propping up. Your self-worth is not tied up in what you do but in who you are. Taking time for yourself and keeping your **self** in the equation is not only important, it is also the key to overcoming the need to please.

KNOWING AND LOVING YOURSELF

"When I discover who I am, I'll be free."

-Ralph Ellison

VI.   JUST WHO DO YOU THINK YOU ARE?

You know the fisherman whose measure of the "one that got away" gets bigger with each telling? Usually PPPs are just the opposite. When they estimate their worth, they often feel half as good as their last good deed or three times (to the tenth power) worse than their last mistake.

How do we get a more accurate measure? If we ask someone else, we can feel uncomfortable and feel obligated to reciprocate. We often discount others' positive opinions because they would never say those kind words if they really knew us. However, any harsh feedback we may receive, regardless of the critic's motivation, is given a great deal of credibility. How fair is that?

Our goal is to begin to be intrinsically motivated (motivated from the inside) rather than extrinsically motivated (relying on others' opinions). In order to do this, we need to increase our self-awareness and intimacy. These exercises are designed to help you begin your journey of positive self-regard.

EXERCISE THREE

Answer the following. If you hide behind a persona, let it fall for the time it takes to answer these questions:

When I am alone, I usually spend my time

My biggest fear regarding my relationships with others is

[ ] I embarrass easily.

[ ] I don't embarrass easily.

When I do get embarrassed, it is usually because

What I believe people think of me:

Ten things that scare me:

1.
2.
3.
4.
5.
6.
7.
8.
9.
10.

How much time do I spend thinking of the things that scare me?

Ten things that bring me joy:

1.
2.
3.
4.
5.
6.
7.
8.
9.
10.

How much time each day I think about that which brings me joy.

If I had time, I would

My anger usually surfaces because

I am ashamed to admit that I

I know my relationship with _____ is not balanced because

I know my relationship with_____ is not balanced because

I know my relationship with_____ is not balanced because

The people I care for most often get:

[ ] my best

[ ] my worst

[ ] too much of me

[ ] too little of me

When you are finished with this experience, give yourself a physical pat on the back or a hug.

Bringing up awareness regarding your need to please may cause feelings of sadness, shame, or guilt. Honor your feelings. Feel them and tell yourself that, *"I learned to be pleasing to try to please others. Now I am learning to care and nurture myself. I am not a bad person. I am just a person trying to make my way."*

What do my answers mean to me?

Regarding my answers, what action do I want to take?

EXERCISE FOUR

This activity may require a bit of discomfort, so take a deep breath and let's begin. Let go of those things that occupy your mind. Tell yourself they will be there when you return from your journey of discovery.

Stand in front of a mirror. Look at your face and look into the windows of your soul, your eyes.
Marvel at their beauty. Is there anything more miraculous and magical than those beautiful eyes looking back at you?
Look deeply at their color and their marvelous pattern.
They are spectacular, aren't they?
Say hello to yourself.
Look at your face. Incredible.
If you begin to pull back or find fault with yourself, not to worry.
Do not berate yourself.
Just go back to your eyes and stare into the depths of you. Then start again.
Do not think of the "beauty" that advertisers air brush into perfection.
I want you to think of real beauty. Your skin is miraculous.
Small pores or large pores—what a wonderful work of art. The human skin is full of receptors ready to bring messages to your brain.
Remarkable.
Your face is beautiful.
Touch your face gently and caress it with tenderness. You are a wonder. Hold your face in your two hands in a loving, grandma-style embrace.

Feel your soft skin. Run your finger along the contours of your face.

Pablo Casals said,

"Each second we live is a new and unique moment of the universe, a moment that will never be again. And what do we teach our children? We teach them that two and two make four and that Paris is the capital of France. When will we also teach them what they are?

"We should say to each of them: Do you know what you are? You are a marvel. You are unique. In all the years that have passed, there has never been another child like you. Your legs, your arms, your clever fingers, the way you move.

"You may become a Shakespeare, a Michelangelo, a Beethoven. You have the capacity for anything. Yes, you are a marvel. And when you grow up, can you then harm another who is, like you, a marvel?

"You must work; we must all work, to make the world worthy of its children."

And friends, we are all children, and we are all marvels. Do not go on until you can see yourself and can marvel at the wonder of you. Breathe deeply and take your time. For some, this activity may bring tears to those beautiful eyes because it has been so long since you have looked with appreciation at you. Tell yourself, "I am a wonder." If you are spiritual, you may want to say a word of thanks for your spectacular self. Give yourself a smile.

Do this activity at least once in the morning and once at night. Practice it until it is second nature for you to enjoy looking at yourself vs. fixing yourself. Do it until it is second nature for you to see your worth and not examine yourself in an effort to determine your ability to measure up. MEASURE UP?!! No need. Imagine yourself full to the brim with love and compassion and self-love. When you are feeling badly about yourself, touch your cheek and remember that you are a wonder. Let's make the universal sign for positive self-regard a loving stroke to the cheek.

EXERCISE FIVE

A-Hoy Matey! This exercise is designed to help you peacefully reclaim yourself. Breathe deeply and settle yourself. Picture in your mind's eye a beautiful sea. Say to yourself:

I am the Captain.

I am the Ship.

I am a proud vessel and do all I need to do to keep myself sea-worthy.

I anchor myself in rough seas.

I know when to call for assistance. I accept assistance with gratitude.

I pull into safe harbors to refuel.

I have everything I need to navigate my course.

I can identify pirates who would take my cargo and leave me adrift.

I take time to breathe the air and enjoy the vistas.

I relish this journey.

Tune into your body's reaction. Imagine the warmth of the sun and smell the salt air. In strength and repose, enjoy yourself.

"Many of us spend our whole lives running from feeling with the mistaken belief that you can not bear the pain. But you have already borne the pain. What you have not done is feel all you are beyond that pain."

-Kahlil Gibran

VII.   THE THINGS I TELL MYSELF

"Sticks and stones may break my bones," but the names I call myself can break my spirit.   People-pleasing is abusive. Neglectful of our own needs and often hypercritical of our actions, we create a standard that is often cruel and unusual.   The words that people pleasers tell themselves are words they would likely never utter to another individual.   It takes kind and loving words and words and words—to repair the damage from which we have been subjected.   Continue staking a claim to your own regard.

EXERCISE SIX

Say to yourself, "I am the expert on myself and can rely on me to see myself fairly and lovingly."

Reflect with gratitude and honesty:

My Most Beautiful Physical Characteristics (write at least three entries):

My Most Beautiful Personality Characteristics (write at least three entries):

If there were no barriers, I would:

What I want my life's work and message to be:

Person (people) who has (have) the potential of being supportive:

Something I wish people knew about me:

I can be a better friend to myself by:

As I read my answers to the above questions aloud to myself, my reaction and/or awareness is:

Daily Recitation: "I am a person worthy of love. Whatever my situation, I will be present to nurture and honor my self."

VIII.   I'VE LOOKED AT ME FROM BOTH SIDES NOW

Speaking of the dark side…are there negative feelings about yourself that are lurking in the dim recesses of your mind?   If there aren't, skip this section and go directly to the section entitled: "Delusion Becomes You."

Let's just face it; we all have a dark side. For most of us, turning the light on our shadow side provides relief. What is hiding under our mental bed is usually not as scary or as big as we thought. When we think of our dark side and ourselves as bad, we tend to invite mistreatment from ourselves and anyone willing to take a jab.

> *"Every one is a moon, and has a dark side which he never shows to anybody."*
>
> ~Mark Twain

So what does our dark side provide us?   Compassion, understanding, and humility. Probably makes us a little more intriguing and real. It teaches us many lessons.

When we hide or deny our dark side is when it has a field day. Things seem to be going along just fine and then BAM! Here comes our party animal to wreak havoc with our persona. It says, "Hello, there. Did someone forget I existed? I believe I will raise a ruckus."

Wholeness occurs when we are able to recognize our dark side and treat it with diplomacy, being neither indulgent nor too critical of it.

EXERCISE SEVEN

Make a list of all your characteristics that you believe to be dark:

How Dark Are They?

Number each of the items on your list. Mark BARELY DARK characteristics with a "1." Mark MODERATELY DARK characteristics with the number "3," and mark VERY DARK characteristics with a "5."

If you have placed all your traits as "5's" or VERY DARK, please seek help. A therapist can either help you work on traits that legitimately need changing or help you lighten your opinion of the traits that may not be as bad as you feel.

Sometimes we need help changing our perspective and our habits. Perpetuating the same old behaviors gets the same old results. Interrupting the pattern may require therapy. If you find yourself struggling, make an appointment.

As I look at the dark-side list and how I have categorized my traits, I am aware that:

What I want to do with my awareness:

Read each of your dark side statements again. Kindly accept that you are a complex individual and say aloud, "I acknowledge and accept all my feelings, and I acknowledge and accept my dark side."

INDEPENDENCE DAY:
The Pleasure is Mine

When thanked for doing something nice, people often say, "The pleasure is mine." To mean it, they have to feel their own strength and enough-ness. Otherwise they might say, "The pleasure is yours, and if you have some crumbs leftover...."

Don't settle for crumbs. Don't wait for perfection. Get out the sparklers. You know the truth; now let it set you free. Mark this day on the calendar. Today is the day you fall in love with you. Celebrate. March in a parade of one. Lay out a picnic and eat corn on the cob. Create a meaningful tribute to the day you declared your freedom.

My special tribute to myself will be:

Draw a picture of how the new you looks:

FINDING
YOUR
VOICE

"It's never too late to be what you might have been."

-George Elliot

IX.   IS IT ME, OR IS THERE SOMETHING WRONG WITH THIS PICTURE?

Trusting My Own Opinion

People pleasers are not always good judges about setting clear boundaries. We may wonder if we are being taken for granted or taken for a ride.

Not being able to trust our own judgment regarding how much is too much, we often become exhausted before we realize we have overdone it. Tired and cross, worn out and discouraged, we pull completely away from those we were helping.

> "A bird doesn't sing because it has an answer, it sings because it has a song."
>
> ~Maya Angelou

While some may intentionally use you, others may be unaware that you have exhausted your reserves. They end up confused. You end up hurt, resentful and wondering if you have "PLEASING" written across your forehead.

EXERCISE EIGHT

Before responding to any request, put it to this test. Circle the number that most closely fits your response.

Level of stress this task would cause:				
[Low]				[High]
1	**2**	**3**	**4**	**5**

Amount of time it would realistically take:				
[Little]				[Lot]
1	**2**	**3**	**4**	**5**

Reasonability of this request:				
[Reasonable]				[Unfair]
1	**2**	**3**	**4**	**5**

Amount already on my plate of responsibilities:				
[Light load]				[Heavy load]
1	**2**	**3**	**4**	**5**

Current level of my energy:				
[High]				[Low]
1	**2**	**3**	**4**	**5**

Current level of my health:				
[Good]				[Poor]
1	2	3	4	5

Level of my desire to be involved in this endeavor:				
[High]				[Low]
1	2	3	4	5

Add up the numbers. If your total is low, between 7–14, this request can probably be done without much sweat. If your total is between 28–35, this request will cost you in time and energy, so you will want to have some very compelling reasons to say yes if you make that choice.

Kindness is not for sale. Ultimately, our goal is to save ourselves AND become as altruistic and giving as we want to be. To do that, we have to be willing and able to say no.

X. NO IS NOT A FOUR-LETTER WORD, BUT "Y-YES" IS

Sometimes it is only after we say yes that we realize that realistically saying no would have been the right answer (EXERCISE EIGHT). We may have underestimated our needs. In the universe, there is an ebb and flow. High tides and low, day and night. A time for busy, a time for quiet. In this time of healing, pulling the reserves a little closer to home is important. In order to do this, you must create a space for yourself. We do that by saying no. Here are 50+ ways to get you started. Practice often. Read the following list aloud:

"No"
"NO"
"**NO!**"(there's three—47 to go)
"Not today"
"Sorry, but no"
"No no na-no-no" (oldies version)
"Not even" (shades of valley girl)
"No thanks" (ah, simplicity)
"I can't" (at least not while I am working on healing)

"Would if I could, but I can't"
"Wouldn't, couldn't, shouldn't" (dash of Dr. Seuss)
"My plate is full right now, but thanks for asking me"
"As if" (more valley girl)
"Not even on a good day" (Clint Eastwood-ish)
"I appreciate your consideration, but no thanks"
"I don't want to" (toddler style)
"Not now, not ever" (dramatic)
"Thanks, but no"
"Thanks, but no thanks"
"Thank you, no" (formal)
"I'm sorry, no"
"I am so very sorry, no" (polite but firm)
"I am not in the least bit sorry, no" (at least firm)
"I am pleased to be asked, but I have to decline"
"I am pleased to be asked, but I have to recline"
"I am not really pleased to be asked, but I am pleased to refuse"
"That's a negative, good buddy" (trucker-ese)
"Nine" (even ten)
"Oh no, no, no" (fifties back-up singer)
"NEVER!" (theatrical)
"Not today, not tomorrow, not ever" (Rhett Butler-ish)
"By all means, no" (confusing but effective)
"I'm quite certain the answer will still be no tomorrow" (Scarlett O'Hara- ish)
"It ain't happening" (direct and dialectical)
"Wouldn't be prudent" (past-presidential)
"Wouldn't on a bet"
  "What part of no don't you understand?" (flip, yet resolute)
  "That is kind of you, but no"
  "Not now"

"Not ever"

"No way"

"Don't ask me" (you won't like the answer)

"I am certain that won't work for me"

"Not on my watch" (or my compass)

"You are out of bounds" (sporty)

"I don't believe that will work"

"Can I get back to you?"

"I appreciate the offer, but no thanks"

"I am trying to carve out more time (more totem poles, more turkeys) so I am not adding any projects"

"Sorry"

"It sounds great (fascinating, time-consuming, interesting, overwhelming) but no thanks"

"I must refuse" (Greta Garboesque)

"I have to turn down (the covers) your offer"

"I must beg (kick, dash, goof) off"

"I'll take a rain check" (and some mud flaps)

"So kind of you, but no"

"I just simply can't"

"You are a dear for asking, but I have to say no" (sweet – decisive- grandma words)

"Please consider me at another time" (perhaps 2200)

"My cup is running over with opportunities (projects, family affairs, aardvarks, liver spots)"

"Positively, absolutely not"

"Thank you for asking; that sounds like something I would really enjoy doing at another time" (like in my dreams)"

"In your dreams"

"While I have to decline at this moment, I hope you ask again in the future"

If you can't say no immediately, say to the person, "I need to get back to you." That gives you time to think and practice your nay-saying skills and put the request to the test (exercise eight). *Remember, you won't always say no. Once you master the art, you get to say yes on your terms and be more likely to do the task with enthusiasm and competence.*

"Be who you are and say what you feel, because those who mind don't matter and those who matter don't mind."

-Dr. Seuss

XI.   ROCKING THE BOAT TO FLOAT MINE
or I'm Alive and They're Kicking

You know, there are those who have benefited from your pleasing.   They have probably enjoyed your pleasing nature. They may or may not know that pleasing has cost you dearly. As you shrug off the part of pleasing that is unhealthy, there will be those who cheer you on and others who wonder, "Who put the bee in your bonnet?" They may think you have become unreasonable asking for your rightful place in the world.

Sometimes it will get confusing.   Sometimes saying no or asking for help or time will make you feel guilty or scared. You will often think it is too much to ask.

Imagine your best friend was asking you for support or help. Would you think their request is reasonable? Probably so. Does it seem outrageous? Probably not. So, be your best friend.

You will have to stand firm, and you may have to negotiate what you need. Challenge your own old, unhealthy ideas. Say to yourself, "Hold it, are my thoughts about myself helpful or hurtful?

I deserve my own kindness and compassion. What can I say that is more productive and loving?

People who will support my efforts:

Something I can say to those who don't:

XII. THE FINE ART OF NEGOTIATION

In their eagerness to cast off their passivity, people often believe that they must act aggressively. The skill of acting assertively requires practice and certainly more creativity and finesse than an act of aggression, but it is very rewarding. In the book, GETTING TO YES (Roger Fisher and William Ury, 1991, p 13), Fisher and Ury describe three styles of negotiators: Hard, Soft, and Principled.

Hard negotiators are hard on the problem and hard on the person. They love to win at all costs and don't mind stomping on you to do it.

Soft negotiators are soft on the problem and soft on the people. They, of course, are people pleasers and may give up a great deal to make certain their opponents don't feel bad. They often come from a battle bruised and empty-handed.

Principled negotiators are soft on the people and hard on the problem. They believe that with dialogue and a cooperative spirit, both parties can get what they need (or at least get close). Being in a dispute with a principled negotiator feels safer and can lead to growth for both.

How to become a principled negotiator and not just a pleaser on steroids?

When you find yourself in a dispute or plan to confront someone:

1. Breathe

2. Ask for time if you get confused or lose sight of the goal

3 Determine what you really NEED vs. what you really WANT

4. Try to determine your "opponent's" needs (vs. wants)

5. Stay calm

6. Neither speak down to your opponent nor take on a younger persona

7. Be creative—try to find new ways to come to a solution. Remember, business as usual gets the same old results.

8. Don't get stuck on issues or semantics. If you need to, agree to disagree on an issue. Then move on to find the best way to work out a solution.

9. Say "ouch" if you are hurt by a comment

It will take practice to become a principled negotiator. There will be those who want to maintain the old rule for fighting. Stay principled. Coming up with a solution that works for both disputants can be very rewarding and can strengthen both casual and intimate relationships.

XIII.   PLAY IT AGAIN SAM—Rewriting the Script

EXERCISE NINE

You will now have a chance to look at past pleasing experiences and rewrite what happened. This exercise is designed to provide an opportunity to practice your new voice. It is healing to be able to rewind and redo. Be creative. This is what you *wish* you would have done. It is important not to edit what you wrote in side B ("Oh yeah, like that would have worked"). Your job is to rewrite the situation AS IF it would work. This is a time for changing the landscape. You will develop your style as you practice.

Side A—How it Was	Side B—How You Wish it Had Been
Write about a time when you were pleasing:	Rewrite the scene from side A, giving yourself a more balanced role in the way you wished it had been.
[Example—sister-in-law assumed I would watch the children during spring break because I did last year. I did it again this year so there wouldn't be any family discord.]	*I wish I would have told my sister-in-law, "Sorry, I'm not available. I am using this time to crash and get rested."] Yes, it is legitimate to rest....*

My reaction to this activity:

XIV. RIGHT MAKES MIGHT

Feel free to add to these lists as you deem necessary:

THE WOMAN'S BILL OF RIGHTS	
I have the right to:	Love whomever I choose
Love my body	Be assertive AND not a bitch
Please ME	Be sensual and not objectified
Feel and call myself beautiful even if I don't resemble the majority of models	Reinvent the wheel
Have the remote possibility	Revert to childhood
SAY NO	Reverberate the rafters
Cry	Recycle a relationship
Be committed and opinionated	Draw conclusions
Sing loudly	Draw strength from men
Whisper, scream, shout, hurt, laugh	Ask for what I need, be picky
Be Madonna (biblical or rock star)	Be enough without children or a mate
Be political	Be fearless, kick ass and take names
Be demonstrative	Know the directions
Be feminine	Starve a fever
Kick box	Feed a spirit
Blow the whistle	Feed an army
Eat ice cream	Feed a baby
Conduct the orchestra or the railroad	Run a marathon, run amok, run for office, run circles around the competition
Be creative	Be a loving step-mom
Be the boss, the expert, the philosopher	Fight in combat (or die fighting for my country)
Be childlike, be in control	Jump to conclusion, jumpstart a battery, jump for joy
Win at monopoly	Order a steak instead of a salad
Paint boldly and/or badly	Expect the household responsibilities to be divided equally
Change the oil, change my hair, my mind, my position, my attitude, my direction	Be tearful and TOUGH
Be raucous, rowdy, prim and proper	Earn an equal wage
Climb trees, corporate ladders, the wall or to the top	Ask for the use of appropriate language in regard to my identity

THE MAN'S BILL OF RIGHTS	
I have the right to:	
Cry	Win at monopoly
Appreciate art	Be able to get lost and NOT ask for directions
Ride motorcycles	Be strong and silent
Play on the jungle gym	Urinate in the woods
Hug my brother, my mother, my lover, my friends	Have moods, be complicated, be mysterious, love simplicity
Sing lullabies, sing drinking songs	Shoot hoops, shoot off my mouth, shoot the breeze
Be great at kissing owwies	Be impatient, cut to the chase
Eat tofu	Love being married, love being single
Be unhandy, be constructive	Practice yoga, my fast-pitch, the piano or what I preach
Love football, hate football, love half-time	Read novels, read faces, read someone the riot act
Be moved to tears, be moved by fears	Be careful, care deeply
Enjoy decorating, organize the kitchen, know my way around the spice rack	Change my mind, be indecisive, be unsure
Love women	Be masculine
Have an opinion	Tune out sometimes
Fold my underwear, do laundry my way	Provide advice AND understanding
Pray out loud and in public	Express outrage and take action regarding gender inequality
Eat steak and potatoes or make quiche	Acknowledge and appreciate the strong female influences in my life
Lift weights and/or bird watch	Hold steady, hold firm, hold babies, hold on for dear life
Be able to get lost AND ask for directions	Feel ALL my feelings and choose to share them or keep them to myself.

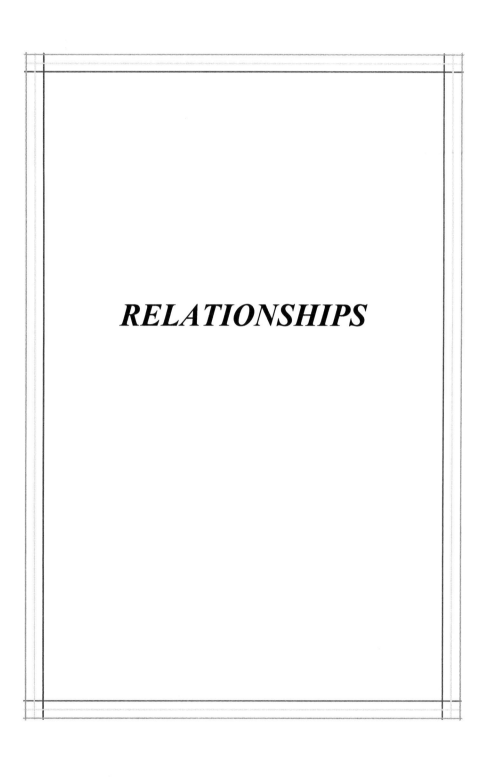

RELATIONSHIPS

"Life is like an ever-shifting kaleidoscope—a slight change, and all patterns alter."

-Sharon Salzberg

Sometimes when we are single, we have no problem being strong and skilled at getting what we need. Then, that certain someone comes along and *BAM!* Our strong inner core melts like a Snickers on the dashboard as we hand over the keys to our heart and allow ourselves to get swept away. Hey, it works in the movies.

XV. BEING SWEPT AWAY—
The Tale of Very Sad Dust Bunnies

You know the fragile web of dust that collects under the couch or an unused bedroom (okay, under my couch, then)? The ones that you usually disregard? The little bunnies that can be easily crushed? The ones that cling to the broom as they are being sent to the garbage?

Let's compare that with being swept away in a relationship. When we are swept away in a relationship, we are fragile. We can easily be crushed. In time, we can be disregarded because we are always there. We become very sad little dust bunnies. And when the relationship is hurtful or ending, we are more likely to cling to the one who is ready to end it all. We give our power and all our sense and worldly possessions away for a warm and fuzzy feeling.

Love is grand. It is wonderful, meaningful, and beautiful. Like the song says, "All you need is love." However, to love is to feel vulnerable. If we do not feel very secure with who we are, we morph in our attempt to be more loveable. The irony is that the object of our affection loses the object of *their* affection.

If you love someone, *you* need to show up. Your loved one fell in love with *you,* not an amoeba (unless of course you are an amoeba—then my humblest apologies). For the rest of us, we should be fully present humans.

<u>Being fully present means that you are responsible for yourself and your happiness.</u> It means that you do not rely on your significant other to complete you. It means that you negotiate and that expectations are shared reciprocally. It means that you believe yourself deserving of a loving relationship. That bears repeating:

> *It means that you believe yourself deserving of a loving relationship.*

It does not mean that you need to parcel out equal rations on a daily basis. Sometimes you will give more. Sometimes you will receive more. It can be messy. When you are fully present, you are able to share more of your true self, be really trusting, and allow yourself a vulnerability that is strong. There is nothing more romantic.

Tips on creating a healthy, happy relationship:

- Keep and foster your own interests.

- Please yourself—it is your responsibility to hold up your side of the relationship.

- Let go of your unrealistic expectations of your partner. It is okay to expect things of your partner and negotiate to get your needs met (see the previous chapter). It is not okay to expect your partner to fill your every need—even if they are willing people pleasers themselves.

- Limit the "we have to talk" conversations to ten minutes, tops. Use "I" messages vs. using "you" messages (*"you should, you always, you never"*).

- Do what you need to do to boost your confidence

- Know both you and your partner's language of love. I highly recommend THE FIVE LOVE LANGUAGES: HOW TO EXPRESS HEARTFELT COMMITMENT TO YOUR MATE (2004) by Gary Chapman. He writes that each of us speaks one love language more fluently than we do others. Knowing my and my mate's language increases the odds that my sweet nothings will be sweet somethings to my partner.

- Be two healthy trees with enough space between the two of you to allow the "sunshine" to shine on you both.

- Share the spotlight.

- Laugh together, play together, and build good memories. These are the investments that hold us when times are tough.

- Ask for what you need. While you may not always get it, it is your right to ask.

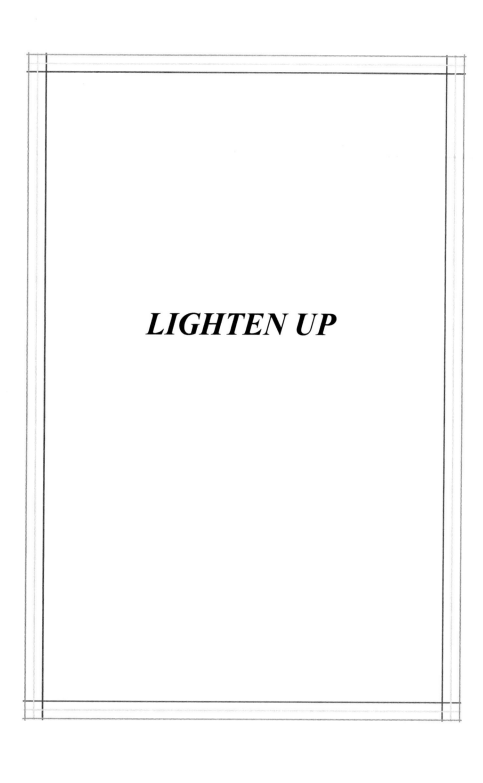

LIGHTEN UP

XVI. LIFTING YOUR SPIRIT

It is hard work to make changes. If done with a spirit of joy and compassion, you can look at your old behaviors with curiosity, interest, and a healthy dose of humor. Your behaviors are ways you have learned to adapt. As you are carving out new and improved behaviors, it is important to keep a perspective that is patient and understanding. Act as a nurturing parent to yourself—a parent who knows that while first steps are wobbly, they are moves in the right direction. With the balance of firm expectations and loving regard, you can make positive changes that last. Loving parents are delighted with their child's efforts and joyful embrace of life.

The chief beauty about time is that you cannot waste it in advance. The next year, the next day, the next hour are lying ready for you, as perfect, as unspoiled, as if you had never wasted or misapplied a single moment in all your life. You can turn over a new leaf every hour if you choose.

~Arnold Bennett

Music, music, music

"Music is a great catalyst for change. Our deepest longings and the language of our heart can resonate on the wings of a song. We can be moved in profound ways.

EXERCISE TEN

Surround yourself with music. Search for great songwriters whose messages are **strong and positive**.

"People don't stop dancing because they get too old; people get too old because they stop dancing."

~ANON

Add to your repertoire. If you are a classical buff, try country. If you are a hip-hop fan, try jazz. If you are a country enthusiast, try reggae, etc.

When you are listening, allow yourself to just be. Sing loudly if you can. Don't worry about the quality of your voice.

If you tend to feel anxious, classical music has been proven to be soothing.

Make up positive lyrics either seriously or in fun. Write a song for children about caring for oneself and caring for others.

Write a song for yourself about saying "no."

Dance with Abandon (or anyone else who is around).

Laughing first, laughing last, laughing often

Did you know that in India they have a Laughing Yoga Day that more than 10,000 people attend? All for the benefits of laughter? Incorporate breathing, yoga, and stretching techniques along with laughter—laughter yoga touts many health benefits. (http://www.laughteryoga.org/about-laughter-yoga.php#, 2007)

Laughing is serious business. Though ancient societies knew the power of laughter, Norman Cousins brought the healing power of laughter to the forefront when he took his recovery from a serious disease into his own hands by laughing. He said that after watching a funny sitcom, his pain was temporarily eased and he just felt better. He described laughing as "inner jogging."

His amazing discoveries led to the development of psychoneourimmunology, or the study of the deep connections between our psyche and the healing process. (Norman Cousins, *ANATOMY OF A ILLNESS AS PERCEIVED BY THE PATIENT, 1985.*)

The study of laughter is interestingly called gelatology (study of Santa's belly?), and the benefits are now well documented.

Evidence is even supporting the notion that positive human experiences like humor and sleep are beneficial in the restoration of waning self-control. (http://faculty.washington.edu/chudler/laugh.html, 2007)

"Try to Remember and if you remember, then follow…"

Do you recall, when we were small, the pleasure of a laugh?

How tears, stomach pain, and an inability to catch our breath added to the enormous fun and grand relief of surrendering to hilarity.

Worries seemed to fade (or become funny) and bodies were cleansed of tension, as we were carried to exhilarating heights and washed back to shore anticipating the next wave.

Once spent, we collapsed as limp as dishrags; our world expanded with possibility and clarity.

EXERCISE ELEVEN

Here are some ways to increase your daily requirement for laughter:

- Read a funny book to a child (Steven Kellogg and Jack Prelutsky are two very funny authors).
- Make it a point to read the comics. Purchase humorous books like Gary Larsen's *Far Side* books.
- Sing a child's song (maybe "itsy, bitsy spider") in the shower like an opera singer (unless you are an opera star…then sing like a cowpoke).
- Watch people.
- Enjoy irony.
- Throw your head back and roar with laughter—don't wait for something funny. Fake it a couple of times and you will soon be genuinely laughing.
- Watch comedies on a regular basis.
- Get a joke book, exchange jokes with a 10-year-old (What do you get if you have 50 mama pigs and 50 daddy deer? *A hundred sowsandbucks.*)
- Make funny faces while you work.
- Smile even when you don't feel like it—it tells your brain to be happy.
- Start a joke notebook.
- Read funny cards in the stationery store, maybe even buy and send one…

> *"The most wasted of all days is one without laughter."*
>
> ~e e. cummings

- Play with an animal. (If you have pets, I bet you have seen your pet grin. Anyone know if cows smile?)
- Play games.

Mediation, Visualization, and my New Dialogue

To change your mind and behavior about pleasing, you will need to focus, forgive yourself and others, let go of old habits, and change your mind. Simple, right?

To do this, you will need time of deep reflection, a quieted mind, and patience.

EXERCISE TWELVE

Marianne Williamson writes:

"Our deepest fear is not that we are inadequate. Our deepest fear is that we are powerful beyond measure. It is our light, not our darkness that most frightens us. We ask ourselves, Who am I to be brilliant, gorgeous, talented, fabulous? Actually, who are you not *to be?"* (Marianne Williamson, 1992, Pg. 190-191).

This exercise is designed to help you stoke your inherent power and peace.

Allow yourself at least 10–20 minutes for this activity. Get comfortable by lying down or cozying up in a comfortable chair.
As you begin to quiet, concentrate on your breathing in and your breathing out. Incorporate all background noise into the rhythmic pattern of your quieting.

Provide yourself the feeling of sweet relief, as you begin to let go of any tightness and residual hurriedness.

This is a vital gift of time and comfort. It is important to your well-being.

Imagine your body as a porous sponge. Beginning at the top of your head, imagine your sponge-self slowly absorbing the gifts of serenity, safety, and contentment.

As the gifts flow into your body, imagine your forehead softening.

Imagine your eyes softening.

Make the absorption slow and easy. Breathe.

Imagine your jaw-line and your mouth softening.

Allow the warmth of these feelings to slide down your neck and over your shoulders.

Deepen your breathing as the feelings of serenity, safety, and contentment move down your arms and onto your torso.

The top of your body should feel light and heavy at the same time.
Allow the flow of wonderful feelings to move down your legs and clear to the tips of your toes.

With every breath, breathe in peace.
Feel the heaviness of your body. Feel, too, its incredible lightness.

Imagine your core as a strong rod that sits next to your backbone and runs from your gut to your heart. Imagine it as strong and glowing. With every breath, imagine you are increasing its glow and its power. *You are strong and powerful.*

As you continue breathing deeply and reveling in your power and serenity, create for yourself a symbol that represents your power. It can be that glowing rod in the core of you, a solid rock, a mountain, a religious item, an oak, a gift you were given from someone you love and admire, or any other image that feels like strength to you. You get to choose this symbol. Imagine that symbol at the center of you.

Continue breathing deeply as you fill your mind with love and regard for yourself. Say, "I am a loving and caring person who deeply loves and cares for myself as well as others. As I parent myself with care and compassion, I feel my completeness. I am whole."

Thinking of your symbol and remembering how strong and peaceful you felt at this moment can help you fill up with strength and serenity when you need a little bolstering during your daily routine.

XVII. "I SHOT THE SHERIFF, BUT I DIDN'T SHOOT THE DEPUTY"

Have you seen movies where the antagonist is the stereotypical sheriff bad-guy, a punitive and controlling slime that seems to swagger even in his car as he drives around town looking for trouble? He is a prejudiced and calculating low-life who treats everyone poorly. He especially judges the hero/shero harshly. One slip up and WHAM, right into jail the (s)hero goes without due cause or a fair trial.

When not paired with a low-life deputy who worships his bully footsteps, the sheriff is ironically paired with a deputy who is his complete opposite—someone who is fair and honest and deeply conflicted by his/her creepy boss.

Liken your harsh inner critic to that punk sheriff—punitive, controlling, and unjust. Okay, so while I am a non-violent person, I will make an exception because I want you to shoot that sheriff's (harsh inner critic's) sorry behind. You do not need an inner voice that keeps you incarcerated. Kick him and that toothpick he chews to the curb. He serves you no longer.

Employ the deputy who is fair, compassionate, and consistent and has high yet attainable expectations by which to set your moral compass. Let no one own you, not even your inner critic. Time is way too precious for you to waste worrying whether you are good enough or if you have a right to your own existence. You are working hard to free yourself from others' opinions. Work equally hard to let go of those old, worn-out tapes in your head that can land you in the slammer.

Ahh, sweet freedom may feel a little empty for those who have spent a lifetime pleasing. If you feel your self-worth slipping, quickly go to the next section and begin to foster your OWN dreams.

"Do not seek to follow the footsteps of the men of old. Seek what they sought."

-Basho

XVIII.   DREAM A LITTLE DREAM

EXERCISE THIRTEEN

GIVE ME 10

Make a list of your talents, gifts, and strengths (e.g., "I am great at…, I am skilled at…, I love to….) You should have at least 10.   If you wrote them earlier, great. They are worth repeating.

> *"Go confidently in the direction of your dreams.*
> *Live the life you have imagined."*
>
> ~Henry David Thoreau

EXERCISE FOURTEEN

GET CREATIVE

All of your experiences in life so far are valuable assets. You have navigated through some pretty rough terrain. The culmination of all you have learned and all you have become helps create a tapestry of complex beauty. Here is where the beauty reaches new vistas. All that you stand for, all that you believe, and the statement that you want to make stretches before you on the horizon. Write down your hopes, dreams and insights.

EXERCISE FIFTEEN

Person of the Year

Fast-forward your life to a prestigious formal dinner. You are at the head table dressed elegantly. The distinguished host for the evening rises.

She says, "Welcome, we are here to honor (your name here) as this year's ***Person of the Year.***

(Your name here) is the epitome of (your best strengths here)

His/her life exemplifies what it means to live intentionally. Our guest of honor has contributed:

We thank and honor our guest. Congratulations!" Applause, standing ovation, tears, flash bulbs...and then you take the podium.)

Your acceptance speech follows:

EXERCISE SIXTEEN

An Interview with Your Favorite TV Personality

Please tell me you have imagined an intimate interview with Oprah (just me, again?). Maybe you prefer Charlie Rose, Barbara Walters, or Larry King. Let's make an imaginary ultra-cool interviewer named Barley Wynking. After being named as Person of the Year, you find yourself invited to all the talk shows. Because you want to continue your pursuits, you have decided to grant just one interview with Barley.

Barley: So ($_{your name here}$), you have just been named Person of the Year. Congratulations! What do you believe contributed to your successful life?

You: Well, Barley, I overcame my struggle with pleasing others and lovingly started telling myself that I mattered and my dreams were important.

Barley: Wow, how did that change you?

You: I began to claim my own sense of self and started to believe that the only limits I had were self-inflicted.

Barley: Yes, that is very important. Your harsh limits were self-inflicted. So, change your limits and you change your life, right?

You: Exactly.

Barley: That's powerful. But I expect it is easier said than done. Can you walk us through the process?

You: Sure. I started to **give myself permission to dream**. And, I was very specific when I was dreaming. In my case, my dream was _____.

Barley: Okay.

You: Then I told three people that I trust.

Barley: Three people that you trust, mm-hmm. So who did you choose?

You: I chose _____, _____ and _____.

I chose them because:

Barley: So…you just told them and nothing else? Explain the significance.

You: Declaring my dreams was the first step to hearing them out loud. And not only did I hear them out loud, I heard them *three times*. Saying them once brought them to the universe as a possibility. Saying them aloud three times moved my dreams closer to probability. Making the declaration to people I trusted was like lifting up the corner of the receiving blanket to present my baby dreams to people who would celebrate and value them.

Later, I would need those folks to give me feedback about HOW to bring the dreams to actualization. I would need to have frank conversations about the roadblocks. That requires a critical eye. Knowing that these three people have viewed these dreams from infancy helped me know that they were pulling for me and were not intent on squashing them. When they had to tell me some tough realities, I knew they were also intent on seeing my dreams thrive.

Staying realistically optimistic was very important to me. It helped me stay determined and not get discouraged to the point of quitting.

Barley: Hanging in there for the long haul is really hard to do, but it so necessary. What else did you do to keep going when things were tough?

You: I started each morning taking time to center myself and taking inventory of what is important to me.

Barley: You mean about your goals or your life?

You: Definitely my life. I needed to bring the big picture into focus and really face the day with a sense of gratitude and surrender.

Barley: Wait. Isn't surrendering counterproductive to realizing your dream? It seems like giving up.

You: While I would like to orchestrate every single thing in my life, there is so much that I do not control. When I let go of those things, there was room for surprises and opportunities that I could not have imagined.

Barley: So it is basically the Serenity Prayer.

You: Exactly. "God, grant me the serenity to accept the things I cannot change; the courage to change the things I can; and the wisdom to know the difference." Using that morning time to center and reflect helped me get my head on straight and focus on those things that I had power to change.

Barley: Hard and profound.

You: Very hard at times. I also had to stop wasting my energy by holding grudges.

Barley: So holding grudges wastes energy?

You: Yes, and it is counter to surrendering. Holding onto blame and condemnation of others for their actions against me takes energy and creates a bitterness that thwarts creativity and positive energy flow. It puts me in a negative power position. It can make me sick and fills me with resentment and bitterness, which is truly poisonous to me and my relationships. It also binds me to the person who wronged me. That can't be good. Forgiving is hard, but the lessons learned and taught are profound. And, the freedom and possibilities expand each moment we let go.

Barley: Way easier said than done.

You: Yes, forgiving is often not a single act but a series of letting go. You forgive and perhaps the "yeah-but" monster creeps into your head. Again you say to yourself, "I choose to forgive." Sometimes I have to say it again and again. It can be rather delicious to be the injured party. There are benefits to being the victim or being righteously indignant. At other times, I may get stuck in the unfairness of the situation. I ask myself, "Why should I forgive such a heinous grievance?" When I can allow the universe to handle such injustice, I receive a gift far larger than I can even imagine. Freedom and grace and depth become my gifts.

Barley: Yes and allows you to move on to the important things you want to do with your life.

You: Yes. The important thing to remember is that forgiving is not a deficit model. It is just the opposite. Not forgiving robs our time, energy, and spirit. Truly forgiving allows me to soar.

Barley: Okay, so you tell trusted people, you surrender and forgive, and then what did you do?

You: That's when immersion starts. I dive right in by learning as much as I can about what it will take for me to accomplish my dream. I want to become an expert on the details—what it takes, what I need to know (and how to get the knowledge), and how to sustain my dream as I go.

Barley: That's the real foundation, isn't it?

You: Yes. Thoreau said, *"Do not worry if you have built your castles in the air. They are where they should be. Now put the foundations under them."*

Barley: So in other words, do what it takes to get it done.

You: Yes! That takes a lot of positive self-talk, self-love, and asking for the encouragement from the three that you confided in. It also takes allowing yourself to not know everything. If you feel you must have the answer to every question, you may not feel free to seek the knowledge you need.

Barley: Yes, we can feel insecure about our not knowing.

You: Of course. In theory, we say it is important to ask questions. We say to each other, "There are no stupid questions" and yet, if we are the ones asking the questions, we can feel vulnerable.

Barley: So how did you overcome that?

You: I haven't! I just allow myself the discomfort. Knowing is better than my temporary insecurity.

Barley: That is worth repeating: "Knowing is better than my temporary insecurity."

You: Yep, so I ask away.

Barley And so you make your way. Is there anything else you have learned?

You: Yes, one more thing. There must be fluidity to my dreams because the dream I realize may not look like my initial dream.

Barley: In other words, sometimes you have to settle for something different from your original dream?

You: Sometimes, but more importantly, sometimes, I didn't have the tools to dream as big as the dream that unfolded.

Barley: I think that's where we will stop. Keep dreaming!

"There can be no happiness if the things we believe in are different from the things we do."

-Freya Madeline Stark

XIX.   OH NO, I FELL OFF THE RECOVERY
WAGON AND I WANT TO PLEASE AGAIN

Okay, here's the deal.   During a stress response, you may temporarily fall back on your pleasing ways.   With love and awareness, your need to please can be recognized and adjusted.

But, if you decide the pleasing life is the life for you, all I ask is that you be the best pleaser you can be.   Here are some pleasing strategies that may help:

1. Never eat dessert in public.   People might think badly about your food consumption.
2. Take out an advertisement in your local newspaper: "IT WAS MY FAULT."
3. Have t-shirts made saying, "I agree with you."
4. Be sure to dress up to fetch the paper from the driveway.
5. Squash that opinion.
6. Have surveys available at your door regarding "ways I can serve you better."
7. Ask servers at your favorite eateries what you can do to make them like you.
8. Have items of clothing made from rugs so that it is easier to walk on you.

9. Remove your chair from the dinner table. You should be at the ready to run to the kitchen at any given moment.
10. Sign up for committees in organizations to which you *don't* belong.
11. Daily affirmations—Ha! Try daily desperations.

When babies learn to walk, there are many self-protective lessons that they, as crawling babies, have mastered. Oddly, these self-protective lessons do not always transfer to the new walker. For instance, the ledge that a baby knows not to try to crawl over now poses a threat for the new toddler. New walkers have to learn again how to navigate some of the same pitfalls from their new vantage point.

As adults, we may have to relearn the pitfalls, too, as we learn to navigate through new developmental landmarks. We may never have had a sense of intimacy with ourselves, or our old intimacy with self doesn't fit the new us. At any rate, there will be times that you won't feel on solid ground as you change. That is normal. And while it may trigger you to want to indulge yourself, allow yourselves a bit of loving discomfort. You can make these changes. I know you can.

To help yourself stay on track, use the activities in the appendix. Do the honoring and feeling activities daily.

Remember that you are beginning a loving relationship with yourself. It takes time and energy, but you are worth it.

STORYTIME

"And the day came when the risk to remain tight in a bud was more painful than the risk it took to blossom."

-Anais Nin

XX.   BE UNIQUELY AND JOYFULLY YOU

Here is a story about Solly whose giving came from abundance and joy.

That's Enough, Solly

When Solly was little, she loved, loved, loved bright colors. She wore bright orange and bright pink and bright green and bright purple.   She loved bright yellow and shocking blue. Sometimes she would wear three shirts at a time in order to make a rainbow of colors.   But when she tried to put on a fourth shirt, Mom would say, "That's enough, Solly."

When she painted, it was hard for her to get the colors vivid enough.   She would put so much paint on one picture that her desk partner would look over at her picture and say, "That's enough, Solly!…   Teacher, Solly is putting too much paint on her picture again."

Solly's teacher would say, "Goodness, your paper is soaked through, that *is* enough, Solly."

When Solly was doing seat work, she would hum to herself. Working and humming, humming and working. When her work was going especially well, she would hum all the louder. The students around her would say, "Teacher!!" and again teacher would say, "That's enough, Solly."

When Solly was a baby, she thought of spaghetti as art. Flung from the tray of her high chair, spaghetti had the right moisture content to stick to any surface... and the joyous orange color was beautiful! With a budding flair that she would perfect as she grew, Solly tossed pasta. Angel-hair pasta, bucatini and fettuccine. As she perfected her art, she moved from pure semolina to spinach and tomato. There were those of a less artistic bend who would try to quash her zest. In fact, throughout her life, Solly encountered many less enthusiastic people than she.

As Solly grew, she enjoyed doing chores. She especially loved doing the dishes in a cloud of bubbles. When Solly did the dishes, she would use extra dish soap. In fact, she would use a lot of extra dish soap. In fact, she would keep squeezing the dish soap bottle until her mother would notice and say, "That's enough, Solly."

When feeding her dog, she would pour a mountain of food in the dog dish. As the kibbles began tumbling out of the bowl, her father would say, "That's enough, Solly."

She had to give up the chore of watering the flowers even though she thoroughly enjoyed it.

Old Mr. Ratchet in the downstairs apartment added accompaniment to Solly's dancing as he pounded the ceiling with his cane. That man had rhythm. Eventually, Solly could hear, "That's enough, Solly," and she would try to settle down and be quiet.

But not for long, for when she quieted her enthusiasm in one area, it would surely pop out in another. If she quieted her feet, she would feel the enthusiasm bubble upward until it found wings on a song. If she quieted her voice, it was not long before she had to make something beautiful from clay or she had to rearrange her bedroom into a theater and act out her latest musical.

The three words that Solly heard even more often than "I love you" were, "That's enough, Solly."

She heard them at school from playground attendants who would yell up to her as she attempted to swing high enough to capture a cloud.

And "That's enough, Solly" was what she heard while helping her mother add ingredients to the cookie dough.

In the school play, she would try to add some flair to her parts until she was eventually told (you guessed it) "That's enough, Solly."

When Solly became an adult, she kept her enthusiasm in spite of some who wanted her to take a quieter approach. Her guests would groan, "No, no thanks, that was delicious but that's enough, Solly," as she attempted to heap third helpings onto their plates.

Her kids liked her energy, but even they would laugh and say, "That's enough, Mom" after she kissed them again and again.

She would hear, "Goodness, that's enough, Solly" when she brought *eight* cakes to the PTA bake sale and still offered to bake some more.

As she grew older, her grandchildren would whisper, "That's enough, Grandma Solly" as her applause echoed in the quiet auditorium, long after the rest of the audience had settled down to hear the next grade perform.

Eventually Solly got even older. Her voice grew hoarse, her restless hands became weak, and her eyesight dimmed even though the twinkle remained. Solly had learned all the lessons she was to learn on earth.

As she lay in her hospital bed very old and very sick, she thought about her life. She thought about all the wonders of the earth and all that remained undone—the places she would not get to see, the words of love she had yet to speak, the songs that still burst forth from her heart that had not yet traveled to her lips.

Most of the time, she thought about her joy, but now as the end drew near, she thought about all the "That's enough, Solly's" she had heard. It made her sad. A tear rolled down her face as she looked up to the heavens and said, "Oh, Lord, I don't think I did enough here on earth. There was so much more I wanted to do! But I tried, Dear God, I really tried."

With a warm embrace, Solly was scooped up to heaven as she heard the words, "That was enough, dear Solly, that's enough....oh.....and by the way, we have an opening in our Heavenly Choir. I hope you are interested."

XXI.   THIS LITTLE LIGHT OF MINE

Here is another story about taking the risk to become fully and radiantly yourself.

LITTLE STAR

Little Star was hiding.

When her mother finally found her, she asked, "What are you doing under the bed, Dear?"

"Nothing," said Little Star.

"Could it be that you are hiding?" asked Mother.

A twinkle of light came from under the bed as Little Star nodded her head.

"Can I come see you?" asked Mother.
Another twinkle came from under the bed.

Mother was a big, beautiful star. It was not easy for her to crawl under the bed. She scooted, she wiggled, and she said "ooff" and "uhhh" before she was under the bed with Little Star.

Little Star giggled.

"Hello, Star Bright," Mother said softly, "this is a great hiding place. By the way," she whispered, "what are we hiding from?"

"Everything," said Little Star.

"Today feels scary?" asked Mother.

"Yes," said Little Star.

"Did you have a daymare?" asked Mother.

"No," said Little Star.

"What scares you, Little One?" asked Mother.

"My light," said Little Star.

"Your light? Ohhhh, I see," said Mother.

"I don't want to be a star," said Little Star. "I would rather be a black hole."

"All that shining getting to you?"

"Yes, and I am not very good at it," said Little Star sadly.

"Well, let's just see," said Mother. "Come on out of here and try with me."

They scooted out from under the bed and sat on Little Star's comforter.

"Okay, give it a try," Mother said, smiling.

"I can't," said Little Star.

"What keeps you from shining?" Mother asked.

"I don't know... maybe others will laugh at me," said Little Star.

"Others may laugh?" asked Mother.

"Yes, what if someone laughs at me?"

"It's a bit of a worry that others like your light, isn't it?"

Little Star nodded.

"Well, said her mother, "along the way, someone who does not understand may laugh, that's true."

"Someone who doesn't understand what?" asked Little Star.

"Only those who do not understand that we need each others' light could ever laugh about another's light. Come on, give it a try" said Mother gently.

"I can't," said Little Star.

"Why?" asked Mother.

"Because, what if my light is puny and does not shine as brightly as I would like?"

"It may not at first, but it brightens every day. The more you love the light, the brighter it shines. Let's see a little shining," encouraged Mother.

"I can't," said Little Star. She hid under the blanket.

"Why?" asked Mother.

"Maybe it will be *too* bright, and everyone will think that I am showing off."

"Ah, but every star has a bright light to show. It's up to each of us to shine as brightly as we can. If it is my job to shine as brightly as I can and your job to shine as brightly as *you* can, then we are not showing off, we are just doing our job."

"What if it hurts?"

"From time to time, it can hurt a little, but hiding our light can hurt a lot."

Little Star was still afraid.

"Shine," said her mother kindly.

"I can't," said Little Star. "I am not sure I want to shine. What if it isn't very fun?"

"Oh, Little Star, shining your own light is the most fun of all. It is not too hot or not too bright or not too scary. It feels great. I have an idea. What if you hold on to me, and we shine together for a while. Would you like that?"

Little Star nodded and came out from under the blanket. She climbed into Mother's arms and held on. Her eyes were tightly shut.

"Here we go, Little Star, I am going to start shining and when you are ready, you shine, too."

Little Star felt cozy in the familiar warmth of her mother's arms. She began to relax. She opened her eyes just a little. Magnificent light streamed around them. Little Star felt proud to be with such a beautiful star as her mother. She opened her eyes a little wider and caught her breath; Mother had never shined as brightly as she shined tonight. Little Star was delighted.

"Mother, you're beautiful!" cried Little Star.

"Little Star," smiled Mother, "I haven't begun to shine yet. The beautiful light is yours."

Little Star looked down at her little self and smiled. She smiled and smiled, and the light around her got even brighter. Little Star glowed. Her mother glowed. Everything felt warm and good and right.

She no longer had to hold on. She hugged her mother tenderly and let go. She unfolded herself and showered the universe with glorious rays. Her mother beamed her encouragement.

Little Star was no longer afraid of her own light.

Tonight, if you look into the night sky, there is a chance that you can see two stars that shine especially brightly. The one on the left is Little Star.

APPENDIX

Taking Your Emotional Temperature

Prescription: Take several times a day.

1. How am I feeling?

FEELING	CHECK AS MANY AS YOU FEEL	BECAUSE:
ANGRY		
SAD		
AFRAID		
GUILTY		
HAPPY		
PROUD		
SECURE		
GRATEFUL		

2. What do I need? (e.g. honor my feelings by feeling them and allowing them to fade, talk to someone, journal, etc.)

HONORING SELF

We honor ourselves by taking care of our needs, speaking up, playing, connecting with others, creating, pampering or challenging ourselves, etc. It is important to do one or more of these daily.

I honored myself today by:

The HALT Method

This acronym is used by AA and other Anonymous groups as a guideline to when you may be susceptible to relapse. When you are:

H̲UNGRY   A̲NGRY   L̲ONELY   T̲IRED

you may feel a strong desire to indulge yourself with pleasing or other unhealthy fillers. Here is an acronym that can help. When your are feeling the desire to indulge in an unhealthy way:

T̲ake some cleansing breaths

L̲isten to your body—am I Hungry, Angry, Lonely or Tired?

C̲alm yourself and take time to address your needs by either eating a healthy snack or meal; using the emotional temperature page to address feelings; call someone, play some upbeat music, or rest.

Identify your go-to fillers. Here are mine:

Hungry—chocolate; Angry—chocolate; Lonely—chocolate;

Tired—chocolate. Hmmm, at least I am consistent.

Create a plan of action when you come to a HALT. Here is mine:

Hungry—sit <u>down</u> with healthy snack. A juicy piece of fruit and small slice of cheese. Angry—go to emotional temperature page—write my feelings, let them fade, decide a plan of action; take a walk and talk out my feelings to myself. Lonely—either call a friend or delight in my own company by getting creative by writing, drawing, etc. Tired—no more quick sugar hits to keep me going when what I need is rest. It is hammock time. I am not a good napper. I do benefit by stopping to put my feet up, breathing deeply and nurturing.

Create your plan.

References

Chapman, G. (2004). *The Five Love Languages*. Chicago, IL: Northfield Publishing.

Cousins, N. (1985). *Anatomy of an Illness as Perceived by the Patient*. New York, NY: Bantam Books.

Fisher, R., & Ury, W. (1991). *Getting to Yes: Negotiating Agreement Without Giving In* (2nd ed.). New York: Penguin.

Kemp, G., & Rosselini, C. (Comps.). (2007, October 02). *Helpguide*. Retrieved May 1, 2007, from http://www.helpguide.org/life/humor_laughter_health.html and http://www.umm.edu/features/laughter.html

Mellin, L. (1997). *The Solution*. New York: Harper Collins.

Neuroscience for Kids: What's So Funny About Laughter and Why: (2007). Retrieved from http://faculty.washington.edu/chudler/laugh.html

Wagner, J. *Lily Speaks*. Retrieved from http://www.lilytomlin.com/lily/quotes.htm

Williamson, M. (1992). *A Return to Love: Reflections on the Principles of a Course in Miracles*. New York: Harper Collins.

About the Author

A therapist and educator, Judy has over twenty years of experience in counseling. She is a licensed professional counselor and has her National Counseling Certification (NCC).

Married 30+ years, she has field experience in creating healthy, happy relationships.

Judy has trained nationally on counseling topics and received the State of Alaska's educational merit award for her work in peacemaking. She and two other colleagues, Connie Hull and Paul Street, received the first Harriet Elizabeth Byrd Award for their "outstanding contributions in the areas of human relations, multiculturalism and/or diversity in the field of education.